C000232900

SU

Ghost

Prepare to be frightened by these terrifying tales
from around Sussex

BRADWELL
BOOKS

Published by Bradwell Books
9 Orgreave Close Sheffield S13 9NP
Email: books@bradwellbooks.co.uk

British Library Cataloguing in Publication Data: a catalogue
record for this book is available from the British Library.

1st Edition

ISBN: 9781909914063

Print: Gomer Press, Llandysul, Ceredigion SA44 4JL
Design by: jenksdesign@yahoo.co.uk

Photograph Credits: ShutterStock.
and others identified separately

CONTENTS

The ancient, creeper-clad Mermaid Inn is arguably Rye's most haunted building. Ghosts have also been seen in the street outside.
Shutterstock/David Fowler

INTRODUCTION

The ancient land of the South Saxons, now called Sussex, is one of the most beautiful and culturally vibrant in southern England. Its spectacular coastline and sunny weather made Sussex one of the first counties to and exploit the 18th-century fad for sea-bathing which began the British love for the seaside. The county's rolling countryside and pretty villages have attracted tourists for centuries and it became a rural second home for the Bloomsbury Group among others. A major portion of Britain's newest National Park, the South Downs, is contained within Sussex.

Sussex is rich in history. Here was fought the most decisive conflict in British history: the Battle of Hastings, which ushered in the Norman age. Battle Abbey, founded to commemorate William the Conqueror's triumph, is just one of the very many important and impressive historical sites to be found in Sussex. The county is especially blessed with castles, some of the best preserved and most beautiful to be found anywhere. Then there are the elegant houses of the Regency period which remind us of the coastal towns' popularity with the aristocracy of two centuries ago.

In addition, Sussex has a rich haunted heritage. Ghosts of those who have lived throughout its long history are said to still be seen, from Saxon warriors, through medieval monks, nuns and knights, Elizabethans and Cavaliers, Regency and Victorian ladies and gents, to even a few in modern dress. Many haunt castles, abbeys or grand houses well worth visiting. Others can be found in the charming villages or out in its glorious countryside.

Of course, today one should not really talk about Sussex as a separate entity. There are two modern counties, East Sussex and West Sussex, between which is sandwiched the unitary authority of Brighton & Hove. However, for the purposes of this book I have embraced the historical, unified county, from which the Sussex spooks themselves date. I hope you enjoy this ramble through one of the most haunted regions in England.

THE HAUNTED RESORTS

The fishing village of Brighthelmston became the busy tourist resort of **Brighton** after the 18th-century fad for sea-bathing brought the nobility down to the coast in droves. When this soon included royalty, its popularity was assured. By the 1860s Brighton was almost unrecognisable. From a population of barely 2,000, it had grown tenfold, with handsome Regency villas and luxury hotels smothering fishermen's cottages and shacks, while a 1,115-foot pleasure pier had been extended into the waves.

Hove was even smaller than Brighton before it underwent its own transformation during the Regency and Victorian periods. Before sea-bathing became trendy, Hove's main business had been smuggling. In 1997 these now substantial neighbouring towns became one unitary authority, the borough of Brighton & Hove.

A 19th-century engraving of Brighton, which expanded rapidly after becoming
the most popular sea-bathing resort of the Regency period.
Shutterstock/ Morphart Creation

Brighton's luxury hotels are symbols of its great success as a leisure destination. Many of them are haunted. The Regency Hotel has two ghosts. One is the apparition of a tall, slender woman dressed in grey. She drifts quietly about the building, sometimes passing deftly through solid walls. It's thought she might have been a former landlady. The other ghost is more tragic, that of a young Victorian girl who fell to her death from an upper-storey window. The legend recounted to explain the accident is that she became frightened when she smelled gas coming from a recently installed gas pipe and crawled out on to the window ledge to avoid being suffocated. People claimed to have seen the fatal fall being re-enacted.

The Marlborough Hotel is haunted by murder victim Lucy Packham. Lucy was killed by her brute of a husband, the proprietor of the hotel, in March 1900. Lucy is rarely seen but makes her presence known by mucking around with the lights and the beer taps and by knocking glasses off shelves. A gentleman in a bowler hat haunts The Royal Albion Hotel. He is believed to be keen sportsman and philanthropist Sir Harry Preston, who refurbished the Albion in 1910. Preston was a dapper little gentleman, described by author Beverley Nicholls as 'tiny, with a mauve complexion [and] rather common'. Doors in the Albion have been seen to open and close without human agency and the lift has been known to go up and down of its own accord.

The Grand Hotel is one of Brighton's many haunted hotels. A shadowy apparition has been seen on the seventh floor but details of its appearance or behaviour are vague.
Shutterstock/ Jacqueline Abromeit

Ghosts have also been reported from the Iron Duke Hotel in Hove. The hotel started life as an administrative building and magistrates' court, raised in 1828 to cater to the rapidly expanding town. A woman with a dog has been seen in one of the bedrooms and a guest woke to find another female phantom – or perhaps the same one – sitting nonchalantly on the end of his bed. The ghost of a small girl was glimpsed by a cleaner near the back stairs.

Many of Brighton's pubs and bars also have haunted reputations. The King and Queen in Marlborough Place was built in the 1930s on the site of an 18th-century inn. Disembodied footsteps have been heard on numerous occasions and members of staff have reported experiencing inexplicable feelings of dread. Something spooky but ill-defined has been seen in the kitchen, too. Both murder and suicide are known to have occurred on the site but, unless the ghost reveals itself more clearly, one can only conjecture on the reason for the haunting.

According to *Paranormal Brighton and Hove* by Janet Cameron, Black Lion Street has two haunted pubs. The Black Lion, after which it is named, is on the site of an old brewery which was run by Deryk Carver, a Protestant martyr who was burned to death on the orders of 'Bloody' Mary I. The ghost glimpsed from time to time in the cellar is claimed to be Carver's. This theory is supported by the fact that the ghostly phenomena experienced in the pub during the course of the year (odd noises, inexplicable moving of objects etc.) 'reach fever pitch' on the anniversary of the martyr's death, 22 July. Further down the street, the handsome Cricketers has a ghostly nun and 'a pale-faced man in a long black coat' among its regulars. In addition, something invisible with cold, clammy hands has made its unwelcome presence known in the ladies' loo.

The Cricketers' phantom nun may well be the same one said to patrol Brighton's network of narrow shop-lined streets known as The Lanes. If so, she may well haunt the Druid's Head, too, for a nun is one of the ghosts seen in this 16th-century inn. Further apparitions include a monk, a smuggler and a woman in a red dress. No less a personage than King George IV is claimed to haunt a subterranean tunnel which stretches from the pub's cellar to the Pavilion (more of which later). I assume it must be a fairly wide tunnel, for George was famously plump.

The seafront at Brighton. The vast crowds of visitors to Brighton and Hove's attractions over the centuries have created numerous ghosts, many in the city's public buildings, such as pubs and theatres.
Shutterstock/ Paul J Martin

The Brighton Rocks cocktail bar, formerly an old coaching inn called The Battle of Waterloo, has a romantic legend attached to it. The story tells of a highwayman who held up a coach carrying the mayor and his beautiful daughter. He promptly shot dead the mayor and his coachman and abducted the pretty girl, who was never seen again. The story ends that the murdered coachman has haunted the inn ever since.

Over in Hove, more nuns haunt the Hove Place; not surprisingly, for it was formerly a convent. The Bow Street Runners is so named because it used to be a police station. A drunken woman who died after being confined to a cell 'for her own good' sadly passed away during the night. It is believed to be her pale face that staff have seen peering out of the darkness. The same ghost is blamed for the number of glasses that inexplicably fall from shelves or smash for no apparent reason in front of startled witnesses.

The 16th-century Hangleton Manor is now an inn. According to *Ghosts of Sussex* by Judy Middleton, there are at least three ghosts at Hangleton Manor. One is of a dashing gentleman of an earlier age clad in a white velvet cloak. The other two are of women. One is more felt than seen. Many have felt her sweeping past them or even gently pushing them. Glimpses of her brown skirt have been seen from time to time.

The other ghost is a strange and tragic one: disembodied arms clutching out of the darkness. They are said to belong to a servant girl who was made pregnant by the lord of the manor. Spurned by him and feeling overcome with despair, she threw her baby out of an attic window. Instantly overcome with horror and remorse, she made a grab for the child's clothes as it hurtled to its death. But she was too late. The shade of the sad servant girl has also occasionally been seen, especially in the days before the manor was converted to an inn and when there were children sleeping in the house.

Another public building which has attracted paranormal activity is Brighton's Theatre Royal. According to Judy Middleton, this handsome building dating from the early 1800s is haunted by a Grey Lady. A wardrobe mistress got a good look at one of these ghosts in 1982. She said it was of a woman 'between fifty and sixty years old and she wore a long grey dress with a tight waist and a full skirt. She had a grey veiling on her head. Her face was very stern and some silvery hair hung in a fringe.' The apparition is usually seen in the area of the dressing rooms.

Haunted Theatres of East Sussex by Tina Lakin (one of the more focused books on haunted locations in Britain I have come across) adds that the Theatre Royal is also haunted by a former doorman who loved his work so much that his spirit lingers here. He can still be seen, resplendent in his uniform complete with gold braid and epaulettes.

The ghost of a little girl in Victorian costume sits at the top of the stairs in the Nightingale Theatre opposite the Railway Station. She is said to have died of a chill after bathing in the sea and dates from the time when the arts venue was still the Railway Inn. At the Hippodrome after closing time a mysterious light is sometimes seen. The small, flickering flame appears to be that of a candle held at shoulder height by someone invisible in the dark. Strange noises, including spine-tingling laughter, have also been experienced.

Brighton's most visible 'ghost' is that of its West Pier. The West Pier is the elder of Brighton's two remaining piers and it closed in 1975. The more elaborate, and longer, Palace Pier still thrives but the West Pier suffered repeated storm damage and, in 2003, a disastrous fire. It has since been partly demolished for safety reasons. Now it sits forlornly in the sea, an iron skeleton, its future still undecided (despite being a Grade I listed building). Its Pier Theatre was haunted by a well-dressed gentleman whom actors and actresses would occasionally see sitting in the same place in the auditorium during rehearsals.

Rumour has it that on stormy nights a vision of the Palace Pier as it was during its Victorian heyday can sometimes be glimpsed. A feature prominent in the apparition is the extravagantly designed Oriental Theatre, which was partly demolished after a particularly severe storm in the 1980s. This rare phantom is now the only way to see it restored to its former glory. Amusingly, the pier's 19th-century Ghost Train is also supposedly haunted. Much of the 'activity' is simply gremlins – unexplained power-outs and the like – but disembodied footsteps have also been detected wandering through the tunnels. The jokey explanation is that the ghost is of a person who died of fright on the Ghost Train's inaugural 'journey' more than a hundred years ago.

Other surprising haunted locations in Brighton and Hove include the Old Police Cells Museum, said to be haunted by a Chief Constable who was killed by an enraged prisoner,

Brighton Pier, more properly the Brighton Marine Palace and Pier, as it appears today. Occasionally, due to some strange trick of time, it is claimed that the Pier can be seen as it was in the 19th century.
Shutterstock/Chris Harvey

and the Sea Life Centre on the seafront. For years the aquarium haunting was a vague one: strange lights, odd noises, the unexplained switching on and off of electrical equipment, that sort of thing. But in 2005 a number of members of staff reported seeing the spectre of a man with a hunched back. One cleaner, who saw it in the main viewing tunnel, said she felt 'a horrible chill' as it passed her. A priest agreed to bless the building.

The accolade of most haunted house in Brighton and Hove is often given to Preston Manor. With parts of the interior dating back to the 1200s, this largely 18th-century mansion was formerly to be found in the village of Preston, which has since been swallowed up by the modern conurbation. The house is now a museum evoking the life of the upper classes during the Edwardian period. Preston Manor's traditional ghost is that of a 'White Lady'. A séance held in 1896 suggested that the ghost was that of a nun, who had been excommunicated and then executed for some past misdemeanour.

When a woman's skeleton was later unearthed in the garden it was reburied in the nearby churchyard. Whether the bones belonged to the nun are unclear, for when the White Lady subsequently appeared to an army officer, telling him she had been wrongly excommunicated, she had no knowledge of having been buried in consecrated ground. Masses for her soul were arranged nonetheless but, since she continues to haunt Preston Manor, we must assume they did not satisfy her.

The house has become popular with ghost-hunting groups in recent years and a further range of spooky goings-on have been reported, especially eerie sounds such as moaning, groaning, a child's sobbing and the voices of adults raised in anger. Further apparitions include a 'grey lady', a disembodied hand floating in a darkened bedroom, and a possible sighting of a spectral dog.

By far the most famous haunted house in Brighton and Hove, however, is surely the Royal Pavilion. The Pavilion was built on the orders of the Prince Regent, later George IV, as a summer retreat and 'pleasure palace'. Orientalism was at its height at the time and the building is a fantastic concoction of Indian-style domes and minarets, with a riot of Chinese-inspired decoration inside it. Samuel Johnson unkindly said of the Pavilion that 'it looked for all the world as if the Dome

Preston Manor is considered by many to be Brighton and Hove's most haunted house. © *Marq English*

of St Paul's [Cathedral] had come down to Brighton and pupped'. Today its extravagant architecture and lavish interior attract thousands of visitors every year.

The pudgy but elegant figure of George IV has been known to promenade in the art gallery. The apparition of a large lady in a floppy hat has been seen walking round the banqueting table as if trying to find her place. The ghost was later identified as that of Martha Gunn, an enthusiastic 'dipper' who helped popularise sea-bathing at Brighton. A little private staircase leading from the King's Apartment is haunted by a spectral servant.

Outside, in the gardens, a much more gruesome ghost has been encountered. This is the spectre of a hideously decaying body, with ghostly maggots writhing in its empty eye-sockets. This is supposed to represent John Robinson, a

*The opulent Royal Pavilion, haunted by the man who ordered it to be built,
King George IV, among other ghosts.* Shutterstock/ian woolcock

mercenary who had his eyes put out for supporting a failed rebellion in the Middle East. He was found begging in the street by an Englishman, who brought him back to Brighton. But Robinson died almost as soon as his feet touched his home soil, in the place now occupied by the Pavilion's grounds.

Prior to the 19th century little existed in the area now occupied by the thriving resort of **Eastbourne**. With Brighton's burgeoning success, however, local landowner the Duke of Devonshire invested hugely in laying out a new town and building everything necessary to attract the sea-bathing gentry (and later, more humble folk). His gamble most certainly paid off.

Eastbourne's pier, in common with those at Brighton, is believed to be haunted. Author Janet Cameron interviewed a member of the pier staff who claimed to have witnessed a range of paranormal activity here, including the sighting of an apparition, apparently of a man in a black cape and wearing a 'trilby-type hat'. Further witnesses have reported strange goings-on in the Atlantis nightclub. The ghosts of a woman in black, a soldier in the uniform of the Second World War and a morose child have been seen. The venue has also experienced weird lights and sounds and the inexplicable behaviour of electrical equipment.

In her *Paranormal Eastbourne*, Janet Cameron has highlighted a considerable number of haunted locations in the town and surrounding area. These include a number of pubs, such as The Lamb in Eastbourne's Old Town, parts of which date back to the Middle Ages. The ghost of a tall man with blond, curly hair has been glimpsed in The Lamb's bar from time to time. A sobbing child has been both seen and heard in the laundry. Not far away is The Tally Ho, where the ghost of another girl makes her presence known in a much more cheerful manner. She can be heard chattering away in various parts of the pub but is rarely seen.

A man wearing 'a big tall hat' is the ghost of The Royal Sovereign, a pub which started life as a police station. England's first policemen wore a kind of top hat. The Brazz brasserie in the Enterprise Centre occupies a former railway shunting shed. After hours a pair of ghosts in Victorian working clothes has been seen on a number of occasions by

A considerable amount of paranormal activity has been reported from Eastbourne's 19th-century pier. Shutterstock/Marcin Sylwia Ciesielski

the owners. They are described as 'the ghosts of an engine driver and, beside him, a small boy carrying a coal scuttle. Their faces are sweaty and blackened from their labours in the engine room of an old steam engine.'

The novelist Pamela Frankau had an eerie experience in 1918 when she was a pupil at a school in Eastbourne called Claremont. The young Miss Frankau was returning to her bedroom and was just stepping onto a landing when something caught her eye. At the top of the stairs there stood a wardrobe, its door ajar. A mirror set into the door happened to be reflecting the interior of the girl's room, opposite. In the mirror Miss Frankau saw the shadow of something scuttling across her bedroom floor. An instant later a small, white, hunched figure ran out of the room onto the landing and faded away before her startled eyes.

The exclusive Eastbourne College boarding school is also said to have a ghost, but this one is more identifiable than the strange thing seen by Pamela Frankau. Tradition states that it is the spirit of an unhappy pupil who hanged himself in one of the dormitories. When the late ghost-hunter Andrew Green visited the school to learn more, staff poured cold water on the tale, stating: 'Young boys are prone to invent stories of this nature.' Nevertheless, a former member of staff told Green she had seen 'the misty figure of a young boy' standing in a doorway to one of the bedrooms.

Andrew Green also highlighted accounts of a ghostly woman in grey which has alarmed a number of motorists at the Willingdon Roundabout in the west of the town. The apparition tends to appear in the late afternoon and strolls across the road with no regard for traffic. A fatal smash occurred at the roundabout in the 1920s and it is thought the ghost may be of one of the victims, possibly a lady golfer.

Green set down the account of one driver who had nearly run over the ghost on two occasions. The witness said: 'I nearly had a heart attack the first time, for suddenly this woman was in front of my car and I had absolutely no chance of avoiding her. But when I finally stopped, with a feeling of horror at having killed a pedestrian, and went back to the spot, there was nothing to be seen. The second time was nearly a year later when I had forgotten that first weird incident, and exactly the same thing happened.'

According to Tina Lakin, Eastbourne also has at least one haunted theatre. In her *Haunted Theatres of East Sussex*, the author states that the ghost of the Royal Hippodrome (not to be confused with the equally haunted theatre of the same name in Brighton) is that of Emily Fogarth, the daughter of a former manager. She died a hundred or so years ago at the age of twelve. Her ghost is described as 'a young girl with her hair in long curly spirals and wearing a rich, deep-blue velvet dress with lace panelling, frilly petticoats and patent-leather boots'. This amiable spook hangs out in actresses' dressing rooms (never those of men), usually making itself comfortable in a handy chair while the performers put on their costumes or make-up. Far from putting off the actresses, the presence of the little ghost seems to inspire confidence.

Janet Cameron adds that Emily is not the only ghost at the Royal Hippodrome. Her fellow haunter couldn't be more different, for it is said to be the ghost of the aptly named actor Tod Slaughter. Slaughter carved out – and that's the right expression – a career playing mainly maniacs and murderers on stage and screen. A specialist in Victorian melodramas of the bloodiest kind, one of his best-known roles was as his namesake: Sweeney Todd, the Demon Barber of Fleet Street. His 1940 movie adaptation of *The Woman in White* (renamed *Crimes At The Dark House*) sees him at his overripe and grisly best and owes little to Wilkie Collins.

Slaughter's final performance, in 1956, was either at the Hippodrome in Eastbourne or at Derby: there are conflicting accounts. At any rate, the apparition of 'a tall gentleman in black' glimpsed in various parts of the Hippodrome has become associated with 'Mr Murder', as Slaughter used to bill himself. The ghost is blamed for any odd incident at the

Tod Slaughter, the self-styled 'Mr Murder', is alleged to haunt the Royal Hippodrome Theatre in Eastbourne.

theatre and particularly for the mysterious sound of a heavy chain being dragged about (shades of Jacob Marley). 'He' has also been known to play the piano.

Yet another haunted theatre can be found at **Worthing**. Judy Middleton describes the ghost of the Connaught as a 'Grey Lady'. The only detail she has of her is that she wears a long, grey gown. Roy Harley Lewis, in his *Theatre Ghosts*, has more to say, although he admits that descriptions of the apparition vary between being a lady in Elizabethan or in Victorian costume. When David Scanlan, author of *Paranormal Sussex*, visited the theatre, he learnt of a sighting of the Grey Lady in which it was noticed that she was 'sporting a 1930s hairstyle'. It's possible they are ghosts of the same actress wearing different costumes.

When paranormal investigator Andrew Green decided to stay the night in Worthing, he found he'd accidentally chosen a haunted B&B. The incident, which he relates in his book *Our Haunted Kingdom*, took place in 1951. He writes: 'I was woken by a young lad bringing in a cup of tea. I thanked him, but finding the liquid cold and horribly sweet looked up at him to make some comment to find that he had gone. He had appeared to be very ill with a small thin grey haggard little face and huge brown eyes like saucers accentuated by dark circles. What heightened his general appearance of misery and neglect was the bedraggled older style brown suit that hung rag-like from his shoulders.'

When he mentioned his experience to the guest house's owners, they were as puzzled as he was, since there were no children in the house and it wasn't their policy to bring cups of tea to their boarders in the morning. They did suggest that the cold tea might have been left there from the previous night and presumably thought Mr Green was a rather confused gentleman who had had a dream. However, when Green spoke privately to the regular boarders he learnt that a few of them had shared his experience on previous occasions. The incident remained a mystery.

Shoreham-by-Sea also has a number of haunted sites, a few of them surprisingly modern. The area of land now occupied by the Co-operative supermarket formerly housed a school and workhouse. The shades of girls in white pinafores, together with a man in a top hat, have been seen here. A considerable amount of paranormal activity has been reported from the Adur Civic Centre, including the ghost of a former caretaker and the disconcerting sight of two ghostly feet, minus the rest of the body.

When wealthy Richard Hotham began to transform the West Sussex hamlet of **Bognor** into a major resort towards the end of the 18th century he failed to get his new town renamed 'Hothamton' as he'd vaingloriously hoped but his enterprise was successful enough to attract royalty. The 'Regis' was added about a century after Hotham's death. King George V granted the royal status after he stayed in the town in 1929.

Arron Weedall recounts a number of ghost stories from Bognor Regis in his book *Haunted Chichester and Beyond*, including accounts of another haunted pier, the fourth in Sussex. Mr Weedall's research reveals that the ghost of 'an old-looking man with dark hair' has been seen in a nightclub on the pier. The historic Picturedrome Cinema, which opened in 1919 when the movies were silent, black-and-white and strictly 2D, has a ghostly cinephile, who strolls about the auditorium and has been known to sit in one of the seats, usually when there is nothing on the screen. Of course, if he chose to sit in the cinema while a movie is showing, how would anyone know, in the dark, that there wasn't a ghost sitting beside them?

A particularly haunted building is Bradshaw House in Sudley Road. Formerly a private home, Bradshaw House now forms two distinctly different premises: one half is a dental practice, the other a nightclub. There are allegedly three ghosts here;

one rather sinister, the others benign. Of the friendlier ghosts, one is believed to be of a former club regular called Dave, who died in the 1960s. The other is a female presence, nicknamed 'Sue', who has been seen sadly watching revellers on the dance floor. An unexpected feeling of despair or melancholy which sometimes descends on nightclub staff is blamed on Sue, who is thought to be the spirit of a girl who suffered a fatal fall from an upstairs window.

The third ghost is described as 'a tall, nasty-looking man' and may be the ghost of a murderer who strangled a girl to death in the house in the 1950s. By coincidence (or maybe not), Bradshaw House is situated next door to Bognor's Spiritualist Church.

Sussex can boast at least four haunted piers, including the one at Bognor Regis.
Shutterstock/ian woolcock

MORE HAUNTED TOWNS AND VILLAGES

Of all the towns in England recognised for their beauty and charm, **Rye**, in East Sussex, is among the most celebrated. One of the old defensive 'Cinque Ports' of England's South Coast, Rye was once upon a time almost entirely surrounded by the sea. It was an important centre for shipbuilding but in later centuries, when its prosperity declined, Rye's main 'industry' became smuggling, especially of wool.

The chief industry today is probably tourism. Visitors are attracted by Rye's 'olde worlde' charm. Lovely medieval houses jostle along narrow, cobble-lined streets which lead down to an ancient harbour defended by massive towers and walls. Rye became the model for 'Tilling', that hotbed of provincial one-upmanship which featured in the *Mapp and Lucia* books of author E.F. Benson.

Rye is notable in being the former home of not one but two famous writers of ghost stories: the above-named Benson and also Henry James. Not only did the authors live in the same town, they also lived in the same property, although at different times. Lamb House is a brick-fronted Georgian manor house with a pretty walled garden. It is now in the care of the National Trust.

Henry James lived in Lamb House from 1898 to 1916. In his first year of residence he wrote that masterpiece of growing supernatural dread, *The Turn of the Screw*. E.F. Benson moved into Lamb House in 1918 and wrote many of his best ghost stories while living here. During his lifetime, Benson's 'Spook

Stories', as he called them, were better known than his humorous works. Lamb House provided plenty of inspiration. In company with the Vicar of Rye, he actually saw a ghost here: the apparition of a man in black near the bottom of the garden. Benson admitted that the sighting 'had not occasioned [him] the slightest qualms' but he still succeeded in working up a scary story from the incident.

Henry James, left, and E.F. Benson were both celebrated writers of ghost stories and both lived at Lamb House, Rye.

In addition to the vague figure glimpsed by E.F. Benson and his clergyman friend, Lamb House is haunted by a woman in Victorian dress, who has been seen sitting on a chair in the front hall. In 1968 and for the next ten years another author lived here, Rumer Godden, whose many novels include *Black Narcissus*, filmed in 1947 and starring Deborah Kerr (who coincidentally also starred in *The Innocents*, the 1961 film adaptation of James's *The Turn of the Screw*). Godden became convinced that the ghost was of Henry James's cook, a Mrs Paddington.

Among Rye's many splendid old properties is Fletcher's House, now a tea-room. It stands opposite St Mary's Church and was the vicarage in centuries past. John Fletcher, a contemporary of Shakespeare, who wrote plays with his fellow dramatist Francis Beaumont, lived here for the first two years of his life. Oddly enough for such a venerable building, its ghost appears to be of someone comparatively modern. He is described as an ordinary-looking, tall young man in a dark lounge suit. This unknown individual was seen on the landing but vanished before the witness's astonished eyes. Although his appearances are rare, another phenomenon is more frequent: the sound of footsteps going up the stairs but made by no visible entity.

The Mermaid Inn is a magnificent, timber-framed and ivy-clad hostelry dating back to the early 15th century, although another structure may have been on the site from the 1100s. It is probably Rye's most haunted building. Its most famous ghost is that of two sword-fighters in doublet and hose who manifest in Room 16. After a fierce fight, one of the men is run through and the other drags the corpse to the corner of the room. After that, the show is over and the ghosts vanish.

Further ghosts include a chubby gent who sits on the ends of people's beds and a young woman who was murdered in the 18th century by a notorious gang of smugglers. In Room 1 guests have seen a female form sitting in a chair by the fireplace. Garments left on this chair were sometimes found to have become unaccountably wet overnight. Outside, in Mermaid Street, apparitions of women in costumes of the medieval period have been seen.

A strange and rather disturbing tale is told to explain the odd name of Turkey Cock Lane in the town. The legend states that a monk, famed for his singing and nicknamed Brother Cantator, became romantically involved, contrary to his vows. The affair exposed, he turned his back on the girl and on normal life. Either voluntarily or otherwise, Brother Cantator was immured in a tiny cell and forbidden to communicate again with the outside world. Eventually, he went mad under this silent treatment and the celebrated singer took to making a strangled, choking sound in his throat like the gobbling of a turkey. This unpleasant sound is said to still be heard in Turkey Cock Lane.

It's possible Brother Cantator's ghost is seen as well as heard, for a ghostly cowled monk has been seen where Turkey Cock Lane joins the medieval Landgate. Further phantom monks – or perhaps the same one – have been encountered in other spots near Turkey Cock Lane and also in Watchbell Street. A particularly scary one was seen in a timber-framed house at the corner of Watchbell Street and Church Square. After hearing weird scratching noises and detecting a dim glow behind a window, the owner went to investigate and was startled to see staring back at him a monk 'with a frightful yellow face' (to quote Judy Middleton).

Lewes is the county town of East Sussex and, historically, of the whole of Sussex. It is also one of the most attractive. The

The Landgate forms part of the medieval defences in the formerly important port of Rye. Near here a spectral monk has been seen.
Shutterstock/David Fowler

pioneering designer and aesthete William Morris said of Lewes: 'You can see Lewes lying like a box of toys under a great amphitheatre of chalk hills … on the whole it is set down better than any town I have seen in England.' In the Middle Ages it was a port. One of the most notable events in the town was the burning to death of seventeen Protestant martyrs during the reign of 'Bloody' Mary I. The tragedy is commemorated as part of the town's Bonfire Night celebrations on 5 November.

Lewes is overlooked by its Norman castle. Unusually for a Sussex castle there are no ghost stories attached to it, but there are other historic properties with a haunted reputation. Anne of Cleves House, south of the town centre, dates from the 15th century and was given to Henry VIII's fourth wife

The slaying of Archbishop Thomas Becket at Canterbury. The knights who committed the murder are said to have had an eerie experience when they afterwards took shelter in Anne of Cleves House, Lewes.

as part of her divorce settlement. Legend has it that it was in this house that the knights who murdered Thomas Becket in Canterbury Cathedral afterwards sought shelter. Supposedly, they gathered round the marble table still present in the house, but when they laid down their swords and gauntlets upon it, the table shrugged them off as if in disgust at the dreadful deed they had helped commit.

Researcher David Scanlan reports rumours of two female phantoms in Anne of Cleves House. One is simply described as 'an old woman'. The other is said to gruesomely swing from a beam on the end of a rope.

Rupert Matthews, in his *Ghost Hunter Walks in Sussex*, reports further rumours, this time of ghostly monks being seen among the ruins of Lewes Priory. He admits: 'There are no reliable sightings in recent years and no details can be gathered. Perhaps the phantom clerics have wandered away from Lewes.' Matthews highlights a number of other haunted locations on his Lewes ghost walk, however, including the town's police station. Here the apparition of a man dressed in the uniform of a police Chief Inspector of the 1950s has been encountered from time to time since the 1960s. Research has failed to reveal any Chief Inspector matching his description, so the ghost's identity and the reason for the haunting are a mystery.

The best-known building alleged to be haunted in Lewes is an unusual one: the prison. HM Prison at Lewes was founded in the 1850s to house prisoners of the Crimean War. It has never been a women's prison, and yet the ghost is that of a woman. The apparition is described as wearing 'Victorian-type' clothing and is said to walk sombrely down one of the corridors. In his *Haunted Sussex Today*, Andrew Green reports a story he was told to explain the haunting. He writes: 'She is thought to be the ghost of a relative or close friend of one of the inmates who, during a visit to the prison, dropped dead at seeing the conditions under which the prisoners were kept.' Naturally, this was in the 19th century, before prison reform. Governors, incidentally, have always denied the existence of any paranormal activity at the prison.

Green also describes an interesting but short-lived haunting in a shop at 4/5 North Street in Lewes town centre. Most of the phenomena were auditory. The spook liked to mimic people's voices, causing confusion by calling out to the family and members of staff. Inexplicable footsteps and the repeated sound of smashing glass, for which there was no physical explanation, were also heard. On one occasion the shadow of a young boy was seen in the shop, but no one was present to cast the shadow. This led to the speculation that the activity was being caused by the spirit of a boy who was killed when a bomb fell on North Street in 1943. The youngster, who was blown across the road and into the premises, was the only person to die in the blast.

Poltergeist activity has been known at The Shelleys Hotel and Restaurant on the High Street. During an outbreak in the 1970s, furniture was thrown around Room 26 and a visiting judge quit the hotel after his bed was levitated three times during the night. The disturbances were linked to a tragic incident in the 1930s when a guest suddenly vanished from the room, leaving his cases behind, and was later found to have gassed himself to death in a nearby house. The apparition of a Cavalier reportedly haunts the top of a staircase and a ghostly old woman in a blue-and-white dress has also been seen in other parts of the hotel.

South-east of Lewes is the exceptionally pretty village of **Alfriston**. Its large and beautifully proportioned church of

The historic and haunted town of Lewes, photographed from its Norman castle.
Shutterstock/Figliola Fantini

St Andrew is known as 'The Cathedral of the South Downs'. Nearby can be found the first ever property to be bought by the National Trust, the medieval Clergy House. According to *Sussex Haunted Heritage* by Debra Munn, a number of spooky goings-on have been experienced in this ancient, thatched and timber-framed cottage. The most dramatic is the sudden appearance of a phantom believed to be that of a customs official (Alfriston was another centre for smuggling). He is described as wearing a black cloak and big boots, with a sword at his hip. More subtle are the sounds of footsteps made by no human agency and the unexpected whiff of cigar smoke in rooms where smoking has been banned for decades. The River Cuckmere flows behind the Clergy House. It has been claimed that a ghostly boat sometimes wends its way up this stretch of the river. It is thought to be a smugglers' barge.

Also near the church is Deans Place Hotel, which has had a haunted reputation for many years. Originally a farmhouse, the hotel has several ghosts. One is a dog that scampers about in the car park or on the road outside. Since the 19th century the apparition of a young woman in a pale blue dress has been seen in the house. One local tradition states that she was the victim of murder. Janet Cameron has collected more recent accounts of ghosts being seen at the hotel, including a figure in a white coat and sporting a tall hat, 'a disembodied hand covered in jewels' and 'a horrible black phantom in the garden'.

The road between Deans Place Hotel and Frog Firle is haunted by the young heir to the wealthy Chowle Estate. He was murdered here in the 18th century while taking his little white dog for a walk. Sometimes the dog is seen rather than the youth.

Alfriston is also blessed with a couple of haunted and atmospheric old pubs. Ye Olde Smugglers Inne, in Market Square, was originally known by the prosaic name of The Market Cross Inn and only became The Smugglers in the 1920s to attract holidaymakers. The pub itself, however, is of genuine age, in parts dating back to the 14th century. Two hundred years or so ago it was the hang-out of a notorious gang of smugglers run by a butcher called Stanton Collins. Some think the ghostly male figure seen from time to time around the pub may be of Collins himself. A ghostly woman in more modern clothes has been known to take a stroll through the bar.

The Clergy House in Alfriston is a rare survivor of a medieval cottage of the Wealden type. Shutterstock/ David Hughes

The medieval Star Inn, Alfriston, has a ghostly regular from a past age

Odd goings-on regularly occur at the beautiful black-and-white Star Inn in the High Street. For example, glasses have moved around unaided in full view of a number of witnesses and on one occasion a cleaner was pushed out of a room by some invisible force. The pub's ghostly 'regular' is a man dressed as a farmer of a past age, in smock and gaiters. He wanders around various parts of this ancient hostelry but is most commonly seen in his favourite place under a clock in the bar. Two ghostly women have also been seen. One is dressed in the elaborate court fashion of the 14th or 15th century; the other in a modest gown of the early to mid-20th century.

The committed ghost-hunter and author Andrew Green, to whom I have referred several times, lived in East Sussex. When he first moved to the county he discovered his new home was haunted. His house, 'Busheygate', beside the A21 just outside the village of **Robertsbridge**, was modelled out of two small labourers' cottages dating from the 1720s. Green's neighbours told him the cottages were haunted by a 'woman in white' and on one occasion Green glimpsed a 'vague shape like a white dress' which 'flitted' past a hall window. The rich aroma of tobacco smoke, where no one had smoked a pipe for decades, was also detected from time to time.

Once in residence at 'Busheygate', Green began to research the ghost stories in and around Robertsbridge and discovered a goodly number. A retired policeman told him about an encounter he had had with a phantom cyclist on the road past Green's cottage. It was showing no lights but when the policeman pulled over in front of it, just before the junction with Poppinghole Lane, he was astonished to find the bike had vanished. He later learnt that a drunken cyclist had been decapitated in a collision with a lorry many years ago along that stretch of road because the bike had neither lights nor reflectors and the driver had failed to see him until it was too late.

Further ghosts include the tragic one of a young girl who was drowned when sudden floods swept down from the surrounding hills after prolonged rain. She was attempting to cross a ford in the Glottenham Stream where a little brick bridge now stands. Her struggling ghost is said to still be seen beneath the bridge in times of flood. Robertsbridge's two pubs, the George and the Seven Stars, have both experienced odd variants on poltergeist-type activity in the past. The latter is also possessed of a phantom monk dressed in a blood-red habit. There is no tradition to explain this unusual mode of dress. It is thought to be the ghost of a monk from a Cistercian Abbey, the ruins of which are a few miles outside the village. The ruins themselves are also claimed to be haunted by more orthodox ghostly monks.

Moving to West Sussex now, and to the village of **Loxwood**, near the Surrey border. Here a vague monk-like figure has been spotted drifting along beside the main road. Sometimes it attempts to cross the road, forcing motorists to slam on the brakes. The apparition may be associated with a monastery which used to stand near the village. However, Andrew

The George Hotel, Crawley, with its distinctive signboard frame, is haunted by an unfortunate night porter. Shutterstock/ Nick Hawkes

Green has an alternative explanation. Loxwood was formerly the base of an obscure sect known as the Cokelers, or Society of Dependents, who were active in the village in the mid-19th century. Female members of the Cokelers wore long black dresses and hood-like bonnets and might possibly have been mistaken for a monk at first glance.

The George Hotel in **Crawley** High Street was formerly an important coaching inn on the London to Brighton route. The Prince Regent and his entourage used to stay here en route to and from the Royal Pavilion. A remnant of the George's grander days is an unusual, hefty wooden frame which was used to suspend the inn sign over the road. Its ghost is said to be that of a butler or night porter named Mark Hewton. Hewton would deliver wine to guests in their rooms and wasn't averse to snaffling wine intended for a guest. He paid for this bad habit when he drank wine that had been poisoned. The guest – and intended victim – didn't touch it, so Hewton helped himself, with fatal consequences.

The Seahorse was an unusual and at one time popular place to enjoy a bite to eat. The *Seahorse* started life as a First World War ammunitions barge; it was then converted for use by the Port of London Health Authority (and renamed the *Hygeia* after the Greek god of healing); finally, in 1984, it was converted into a floating restaurant and stationed in **Littlehampton** marina. Soon after it was opened, weird things began to be noticed aboard the *Seahorse*, especially by a nightwatchman named Chris Schwar. One warm summer's night Mr Schwar became aware of an unseasonal chill. It grew more apparent: there was something deathly about it. And it was accompanied by a feeling of dread bordering on terror. He retreated to a corner and huddled there, shivering and unaccountably scared, until suddenly, it was gone – the night was calm and balmy once again.

Other strange phenomena included mysterious shadows, apparently of a group of people, moving on the wall of the bar, which was empty except for the witness; doors inexplicably opening and closing; and the apparition of 'a person of short stature' which was glimpsed near the kitchen. During its career as the *Hygeia*, the barge was used to get quick assistance to accident victims on board ships and to check whether sick seamen were carrying infectious diseases. It's possible some unfortunates died aboard the *Hygeia*. The

THE GRANDER HAUNTED HOUSES

The foremost haunted house in Sussex is **Brede Place**, a few miles north of Hastings. Brede is a 14th-century stone manor house built for a knight of Edward III's court. The legend attached to the house is a particularly grim one. It claims that Brede was formerly the home of a cannibal: the gigantic Sir Goddard Oxenbridge, who had the habit of eating babies. Eventually, the outraged villagers ganged up on the monstrous Sir Goddard and executed him in a suitably horrible manner. They sawed in half his enormous bloated body at a place called Groaning Bridge. Afterwards, it was said, 'various parts of the luckless giant would appear in different parts of the house'. There is nothing to substantiate the yarn. Ghost-hunter Peter Underwood believes it was invented by smugglers in the 18th century to keep people away from the house after dark.

Stephen Crane, the young author of *The Red Badge of Courage*, lived at Brede in the closing years of the 19th century. He wrote a farcical play based on the idea of the fiendish Sir Goddard returning as a ghost. A group of his literary friends, including Henry James, H.G. Wells and Joseph Conrad, performed it here in 1899.

Whether or not the monstrous baby-eater haunts Brede Place, the house can boast many other ghosts. These include a woman in Elizabethan costume, complete with ruff, and a maid named Martha who was hanged in the grounds after

Ancient and very haunted Brede Place, as illustrated by F.L. Griggs in Highways and Byways in Sussex, published in 1904.

being caught stealing. The chapel is haunted by the headless Father John, a priest who may have died during the persecution of Catholics during the reigns of Henry VIII or Elizabeth I. During the Second World War, Brede Place was used as a garrison for soldiers. Officers reported seeing ghostly monks and experiencing furniture being shifted about as if by invisible hands.

Cuckfield Place, better known now as **Cuckfield Park**, near Haywards Heath, was built in the 16th century to replace a smaller medieval hall. The house and grounds allegedly became haunted a few hundred years later by the spirit of a former owner, Ann Sergison, who died in 1848. Despite passing away at the ripe old age of 85, Ann was a decidedly spirited ghost, not above swinging on the gates into the park and frightening passers-by. In life she had always been, shall we say, a strong character, much given to lawsuits and quarrelling with her neighbours. Indeed she earned the name 'Wicked Dame Sergison' in the district. Three members of the clergy were summoned to deal with the spook and they succeeded in quelling its wayward behaviour by submerging it in the font.

That the splendid **Cowdray House**, near Midhurst, should now be found in ruins might be considered proof of the terrible curse that fell upon it in the 16th century. During the Dissolution of the Monasteries, the owner of Cowdray, Sir Anthony Browne, evicted all the monks then in residence at Battle Abbey. Browne was promptly cursed by one of the disgruntled monks. As he was being booted off the premises he cried out: 'By fire and by water thy line shall come to an end and it shall perish out of the land!'

The curse took some time to come into effect – more than two hundred years, in fact. In 1793 disaster – indeed several disasters – struck. Cowdray was being redecorated in time for the wedding of Sir Anthony's descendant, the Viscount Montague, but a spark from a brazier started a blaze that left the grand house in ruins. While this calamity was occurring, the bridegroom-to-be was enjoying his last few weeks as a bachelor with a friend in Germany. The young viscount was a bit of a daredevil and he and his friend unwisely attempted to shoot some rapids in the River Rhine, with the result that both of them drowned. The curse had come upon Cowdray through the mediums of fire and water, as predicted. The next heir was a childless Catholic priest. His two nephews, who inherited Cowdray on his death, were also drowned, at Bognor. This line of the Browne family had now been extinguished and Cowdray has remained a ruin.

When David Scanlan visited the remains of Cowdray House while researching his *Paranormal Sussex*, he learnt of at least two ghosts. One is said to be the wife of the fifth Viscount Montague, who shot dead a priest for having the temerity of starting Mass without him. He spent the remainder of his life in hiding, ironically enough in a priest hole. The ghost of his long-suffering wife is seen walking towards Cowdray from Midhurst. Between the ruined mansion and the new Cowdray House (the present home of Lord and Lady Cowdray) there is a path which has become known as Lady's Walk after the ghost which patrols it. She is believed to be the widow of the cursed Sir Anthony Browne. Browne himself may have haunted his former bedroom, but the haunting came to an end with the fire.

Eridge Castle, near Eridge Green, was constructed in 1938, on the site of a 16th-century hunting lodge. The grounds are said to be haunted by the ghost of a teenage parlourmaid who hanged herself from a beam in one of the barns after discovering she had become pregnant by her employer. A farm worker who saw the ghost described it as 'a mist in the shape of a young woman'. He watched as it drifted through the barn, vanishing below the centre cross beam.

Cowdray House as it looked in the early 1900s, before it was rescued by the heritage trust now in charge of it.

The wonderfully named **Filching Manor**, near Wannock, is a splendid timber-framed manor house dating from about 1450. A spectral monk has been seen near the entrance and on the road outside. The ghost may have some connection to an ancient abbey which was once situated about two miles away from Filching Manor. The other ghosts of the house are not seen but instead assault the other senses. The first is the unmistakable aroma of pipe smoke, discernible in the dining room where no one is permitted to smoke. The other is the sound of a woman's voice accompanied by a loud clanging, perhaps of a bucket. The phenomenon is heard in the undercroft. Unfortunately, the woman's words are too indistinct to afford an explanation for this unusual haunting.

Bateman's, near Burwash, is a charming stone-built manor house dating from the 17th century. From 1902 till his death in 1936, Bateman's was the home of Rudyard Kipling. The shade of the *Jungle Book* author has been seen on a number of occasions in his study, staring out of the window with a fixed expression, as if he was thinking over a plot or struggling for just the right phrase. The apparition of his widow, Carrie, who continued to live in Bateman's after Kipling's death and who donated it to the National Trust on the stipulation that the study be kept just as her husband left it, has been seen in the grounds. A few years after moving into Bateman's, Kipling wrote a novella entitled *They*, about a couple moving into a house and finding that ghostly children still inhabit it. Bateman's still has something of that atmosphere.

The composer Hubert Parry moved to Rustington in 1880 in order to benefit from the sea air. He had a house especially built for him and it was named **Knightscroft**. Some of Parry's best-known works, including his musical setting of William Blake's poem *Jerusalem*, were composed at Knightcroft. Parry died in 1918. Shortly after moving in, the subsequent owner of Knightscroft was startled to see the unmistakable form of Hubert Parry walk out of a wall. The ghost seemed to look about him with satisfaction, then vanished. The witness said it was just as if Parry was taking one last look at his home before moving on.

The shade of author Rudyard Kipling has been seen in his former home, Bateman's.
Shutterstock/ Nicku

Arron Weedall, author of *Haunted Chichester and Beyond*, has noted a number of interesting haunted houses in West Sussex. These include the charming **Brookpits Manor** at Climping, a 16th-century house faced with knapped flints. In the 1920s Brookpits was used by its owner to accommodate his estate workers, one of whom saw a ghost sitting very much at home in an old chair in the living room. The witness described the apparition as that of 'a large, thick-set man with light-coloured beard, wearing dark clothes including a cape and tall, stovepipe hat'. After a few moments, it melted away. Fifty years later, during extensive restoration work, builders saw a different ghost in the same room, this time of a young girl. She would walk in through a bricked-up window. When this partition wall was removed, the ghost girl's visits ceased.

The National Trust property of **Uppark** has been lovingly restored at great expense after it was largely gutted by fire in 1989. It's a grand Georgian mansion with celebrated landscaped gardens. The Red Room is believed to be haunted by a former owner, Sir Harry Fetherstonhaugh, who sits in a corner quietly observing the visitors. His spirit seems to be fussy about a fire screen which is positioned directly below a portrait made of him when he was a young man. When the screen was set up incorrectly, it was found to have been moved the right way round by the following morning. On a subsequent occasion, the screen was taken away for repair and replaced by a table fitted with its own fire screen. Every morning this was invariably found to have been lowered and it had to be wedged open to stop it being lowered again.

Lavington House, at East Lavington, near Graffham, has a rather more unsavoury ghost. It is said to be of Garton Orme, an 18th-century squire who had more than just an eye for the ladies. After the hasty burial of his wife, who he claimed had died of an infectious disease in order to prevent people from taking too good a look at her corpse – rather suspicious! – he married the rector's daughter and then continued his womanising ways unabated. Even death failed to deter Garton Orme. After his own burial in 1754, his ghost was said to chase women round the churchyard. Female members of the family who moved in after Orme's demise were often startled to have their bottoms pinched by an invisible hand – and they had no doubts as to who was to blame.

Finally, we must consider Priory Farm (formerly **Warbleton Priory**), at Rushlake Green. This ancient farmhouse is the only example of a 'skull house' in Sussex. There are a number of old homes dotted around the British Isles in which a skull is kept on prominent display. In most examples tradition states the skull is of someone with a strong connection to the property, although examination sometimes discredits this. Great importance is placed on the skull remaining in the house; on its removal misfortune would be bound to follow, and the spirit associated with the artefact would disturb the place with mysterious lights, bangs and other paranormal mayhem. Warbleton Priory possessed not one but two skulls but they were stolen in the early 1900s. The fact that no dire consequences occurred as a result rather undermined the legend.

Tradition stated that the skulls belonged to a former owner of the house and the man who murdered him and that they had to be kept together to prevent the troubled spirits from haunting the residents. In his *Gazetteer of British Ghosts*, Peter Underwood goes on to explain: 'Years ago when one of the thick walls of the house was being knocked down, workmen are said to have found the two skulls. When the first was discovered it was buried but the following morning the skull is reputed to have worked its way out of the earth and was found on the doorstep of the farmhouse. The skull was then

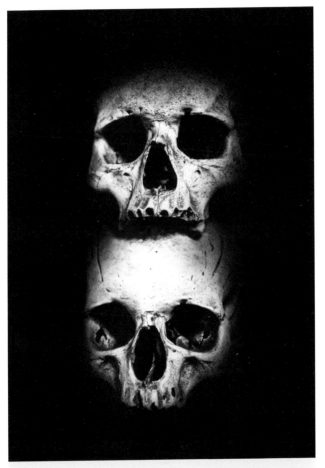

The skulls of a murderer and his victim were formerly kept at Priory Farm and many strange tales were told about them. Shutterstock/ igor.stevanovic

placed in a box and stored on the cross-beams of the house. Later it was placed on a Bible in the front-room where it remained for many years. The second skull was also preserved here for many years and then it turned up at a farmhouse some six miles away where the farmer is said to have been plagued with a whirlwind when he tried to bury it.'

The skulls may originally have had some connection with the now vanished Augustinian monastic house after which Warbleton Priory was named. They may even have been prehistoric, as some of those on display in other houses have proved to be. In support of the murder story is another spooky remnant formerly on show: an indelible bloodstain marking where the deed was done and which refused to be

Warbleton Priory farmhouse, sketched by Charles Harper for his 1907 book on Haunted Houses.

washed away for years and years afterwards. Peter Underwood also records another strange phenomenon from Warbleton Priory. 'On certain moonlit nights,' he wrote, 'a pair of ghostly white hands were said to be seen fluttering at a small window high up near the roof.'

CREEPY CASTLES

Sussex is blessed with a number of spectacular castles and they all appear to be haunted. **Bodiam**, for example, is the archetypal castle with its massive stone walls and crenellated towers rising out of a moat. Moats which still contain water are rare now in Britain. This romantic ruin has been used in many movies and television dramas and is now in the care of the National Trust. People walking past the castle at night have heard singing emanating from within its walls (behind which there is merely a hollow shell). Its most frequently seen ghost is that of a woman peering out of a window in one of the towers. Rupert Matthews, in his *Ghost Hunter Walks in Sussex*, quotes a sighting from 2001:

'At first I just thought she was a visitor,' recalled the witness, 'but then I realised it was getting late and the castle must be closed, so I looked more closely. She was standing quite still, dressed in a long cloak or dress that I think was a pale blue sort of colour. Then she was gone. She did not duck down or climb down the stairs. Just gone.'

Although the phantom lady's dress is here described as 'pale blue', the ghost is referred to as a 'red lady' in Richard

Bodiam Castle, whose classic appearance has made it the star of many a film, has at least two ghosts. © National Trust/Matthew Antrobus

Jones's *Haunted Castles of Britain and Ireland*, which suggests there are either two ghosts or just one who is able to enjoy a change of clothes from time to time. The apparition of a young boy has been seen on the bridge which crosses the moat. He is barefooted and wears an outfit of an earlier time, 'a short jacket or jerkin over trousers that reach to just below the knee'. The little ghost potters over the bridge from the castle but always vanishes before he reaches the dry land.

Even grander is **Herstmonceux Castle**. Herstmonceux, near Hailsham, is a fairytale concoction of 15th-century brickwork. It too rises out of a moat and is surrounded by six hundred acres of grounds which include an Elizabethan formal garden. The castle is privately owned but open to the public. Found within is a room called Drummer's Hall, a reference to the paranormal sound of a drum which used to beat out a tattoo in the dead of night. This is not the only example of a phantom drummer in the UK and usually they are believed to sound only when a death or other calamity is about to befall the household. The drummer of Herstmonceux seems to have had no such purpose. Perhaps it was a natural phenomenon caused by subterranean water or, as at Brede Place in the previous chapter, it was a ruse by smugglers to scare off the curious (there was a lot of smuggling going on in Sussex in the 18th century, as you have probably gathered!).

Calamity did befall Herstmonceux in the 16th century. In 1541 the third Lord Dacre, just seventeen years old, decided it would be good fun to poach some deer from the neighbouring estate of Sir Nicholas Pelham. He and his young friends had been drinking all night and the attempt can hardly have been a serious one. Their blundering about soon alerted Pelham's foresters, who waylaid them in a wood. A fight broke out and one of the gamekeepers was killed, although who by remained unclear. One might have expected Lord Dacre's position to have saved him from prosecution in those lawless days but unfortunately for him, the Dacre family had been at odds with their bad-tempered monarch King Henry VIII for some time. Henry made sure the young lord was found guilty. He was hanged at Tyburn in London and the king promptly claimed the estate.

Lord Dacre's ghost has been seen approaching the castle mounted on a magnificent stallion. Witnesses have noticed his rust-coloured cloak and shining brass spurs. The steed makes a mighty leap into the moat and he and his ghostly rider are seen no more.

Magnificent Herstmonceux Castle, which is haunted by a mysterious drumming noise and several apparitions.
Shutterstock/ rosesmith

Two female phantoms also haunt Herstmonceux. One is the White Lady. Richard Jones states that this is the ghost of a young woman who was raped and murdered by a former lord of the castle. The unfortunate girl made a bid for freedom in the moat and, according to Jones, her spectral form has been seen floundering in the water. Judy Middleton tells a different story. In her *Ghosts of Sussex*, she says that in life the White Lady was Georgiana Naylor, a beauty of the late 18th century. Georgiana seems to have been obsessed with white, dressing in white gowns draped in a white cloak, and riding round the park on a white donkey followed by a pet white doe. Georgiana suffered a misfortune – one possibility being that she was disfigured by a savage dog – and afterwards lived in seclusion abroad. But her ghost has returned to the place she loved, still dressed in her trademark white.

The Grey Lady dates from the following century. In contrast to the proud and beautiful White Lady, hers is a humble and sorrowing ghost, however. She is believed to have been Grace Pelham, who died of self-enforced starvation, in an attempt, it is thought, to ensure she could fit into the tight corsets fashionable in the mid-19th century. Grace's sickly-looking apparition has been in the courtyard, pitifully wringing its hands.

One of the best preserved of the Sussex castles is **Amberley**. Its imposing gate-tower and sixty-foot-high curtain wall were raised in the 14th century by one Bishop Reede. It started life as a fortified home for a succession of Bishops of Chichester. Prior to the Civil War it fell into the possession of the Crown and later on became the home of the Duke of Norfolk. In 1989 it was converted into a luxury hotel, a role it still enjoys to this day.

The ghost story of Amberley Castle is, alas, like so many others, telling of a young maidservant seduced by her employer and abandoned on becoming pregnant. In this case the wrongdoer was a bishop. There are one or two versions of what then happened to the unfortunate girl. One is that she died in childbirth, the other that she threw herself – or was pushed – from the curtain wall. Her unhappy little wraith has been seen in the region of the old kitchens, where she used to work, or high up on the walls, where she keeps a sad watch on the castle's comings and goings.

Much less remains of **Bramber Castle**, a former fortress of the de Breose or de Braose family (either spelling seems acceptable). There are so many tragic tales attached to the castles and grand houses of Sussex that I feel I must apologise for recounting yet another. Bad King John became suspicious of the powerful William de Breose and, in order to ensure his loyalty, he demanded his children as hostages. The family fled to Ireland to escape the cruel command but their bid for freedom failed and the youngsters were incarcerated in Windsor Castle. There they suffered a long, slow death from starvation.

Around Christmas time, it is said, the distressing sight of a little boy and girl, emaciated and dressed in rags, can be seen among the ruins of their former home. Sometimes they would venture into the lane past Bramber Castle, even into the village of Bramber itself, their hands outstretched as if begging for food. Once they had latched on to a passer-by, their pathetic, hollow-cheeked forms would pursue him through the dark, with desperation in their big, imploring eyes. Once spoken to, however, they would turn away and disappear.

Nothing remains of **Verdley Castle**, at Fernhurst, West Sussex, other than a few tree-covered humps and bumps. However, there are rumours that the spooky sounds of 'revelling' have being heard coming from the woods. Presumably this sounds distinctly medieval rather than a modern rave. An old tradition has it that the last bear in England was killed near Verdley Castle and its great, lumbering ghost still haunts the site.

Another ghostly animal haunts **Old Knepp Castle** at West Grinstead (not to be confused with the more recent Knepp Castle, a Georgian manor house and estate now largely given over to wildlife conservation). There is a tale told about Old Knepp Castle that a retainer of King John tried to seduce a local girl, and when she spurned his advances he resorted to a witch to punish her. The witch turned the girl into a white doe and herself into a huge hound, so that she could chase her round and round the park, giving her no rest. The spurned lover ordered his men never to hunt the white doe but one harsh winter a young soldier finally succumbed to temptation. He sent an arrow flying into the deer and another one into the hound that was chasing it. Thus the bewitched girl and her tormentor both died.

During particularly cold winters, after snow has fallen, it is said spots of blood mysteriously appear in the place where the enchanted doe and hound fell. The ghostly form of the white doe may still be seen from time to time, placidly nibbling the grass around the Norman motte where Old Knepp Castle formerly stood.

There are persistent accounts of a ghostly woman being seen in the vicinity of **Hastings Castle**. She is often described as a nun but also as a woman wearing a brown hood and cloak. One witness who saw the figure near the castle's south-facing wall said that it appeared to be carrying a bundle suspiciously reminiscent of a baby. Would a nun be carrying a baby? If she was, there might be a hint here of a drama to explain the haunting, for a nun would have been seriously in breach of her vows if she had been romantically involved with anyone. In 1976 a rector's wife claimed to have got a good enough look at the ghost so as to be able to identify her as Agnes Silby, the lover of a 14th-century dean of the chapel in the castle.

However, opinions remain divided and there is a local tradition that identifies the ghost as that of the jilted girlfriend of a Victorian fisherman. She was abandoned by the man on becoming pregnant (the same sad story) and her ghost is to be seen disposing of the illegitimate child. After ridding herself of the baby, she then did away with herself

The West Sussex town of Arundel boasts many ghosts. Its skyline is dominated by two grand buildings, the 19th-century cathedral and the 11th-century **Arundel Castle**, both of which are haunted (more on the cathedral in the next chapter). The castle is the ancestral seat of the Dukes of Norfolk. Its best-known ghost is that of a humble kitchen boy, who was overworked and harried to death by his tyrannical, cruel master. Local legend has it he can still be heard banging and crashing invisible pots and pans about as he endlessly continues his labours. We have encountered some real horror stories so far in these pages but the idea of being condemned to do the washing up for all eternity strikes me as particularly depressing.

Standing in splendid isolation is the so-called Hiorne Tower, built during a modernisation programme in the 18th century to designs by architect Francis Hiorne. Despite its comparative youth, the tower looks as authentically medieval as the rest of the buildings. The Hiorne Tower is haunted by a suicide, a girl, who, after a failed love affair, climbed to the very top and then threw herself off. The desperate deed has been seen to replay itself, with visitors horrified to see the young woman's body plummeting to the ground.

The 'Blue Man' potters peacefully among the books in Arundel Castle's glorious Gothic library. His identity is a

Arundel Castle was built in the 11th century and then given a suitably Gothic makeover in the 18th century. Its ghosts are legion.
Shutterstock/ Grettchen

mystery but those who have encountered him say he resembles an officer in the Royalist army of the early 17th century. The castles.org website lists two more ghosts of Arundel Castle, one being the shade of the castle's Norman builder, Earl Rodger de Montgomery. The other was seen in the servant's quarters by a footman in training in 1958. He was walking down a ground-floor passage at about 11pm in order to switch off the drawbridge lights.

'I was halfway along,' he recalled, 'when I was physically aware of something in front of me, about fifteen feet away, going in the same direction. As I got nearer I could see the head and shoulders of a man wearing a light grey tunic with loose sleeves. He had long hair and was, I think about 24 years old. The image was like that of an old photo, with the outline blurred. Because of the poor light I could see nothing below waist level. As I walked on, the strong impression seemed to fade and he had gone. He was there only for about half a minute I should think.'

Finally, there is the superstition that a small white bird flaps at the castle windows before an impending death in the family of the Dukes of Norfolk. Belief in ominous 'corpse birds' is a fairly widespread tradition throughout the UK.

Pevensey Castle on the East Sussex coast is wonderfully ancient and full of history. Much of what you see was built by the Romans in the fourth century. It was taken over by the Britons and became part of the 'Saxon Shore' line of defences. The castle also saw the first battle of the Norman Conquest, for it was in Pevensey Bay that William landed his invasion fleet in 1066. After the Conquest, the Normans built a massive keep and further fortifications within the existing structure, using the walls of the Roman fort as an outer curtain wall.

Pevensey Castle is haunted by its past battles. The sounds of fighting, the yells of men and the clashing of swords, have been heard echoing from the stone walls after dark. Phantom soldiers have also been seen marching towards the castle across the marshes from the sea. They are believed to date from a failed attempt by William Rufus to take Pevensey during a rebellion in 1088. A Roman centurion has also been glimpsed patrolling the oldest part of the fort. In common with Herstmonceux, there are also reports of a ghostly drummer still beating his drum.

The ruin's most persistent ghost is that of Lady Jane Pelham, seen strolling along the battlements. While her husband was away fighting in Yorkshire during the reign of Richard II, Lady Jane successfully took command of Pevensey when it became besieged by supporters of Henry Tudor. David Scanlan puts forward an alternative identity for the ghost in his *Paranormal Sussex*, arguing that it might be of Queen Joanna of Navarre, wife of Henry IV and stepmother to Henry V. Henry V accused Joanna of being a witch and had her held prisoner in Pevensey Castle for three years.

If I might make a quick diversion, it would be a shame not to mention the 14th-century **Old Mint House** in Pevensey village. Now an antiques shop, this medieval mansion started life as a Norman mint and then became home to Andrew Borde, Henry VIII's physician. In 1586, after Borde's time, a double murder is believed to have taken place in a room on the ground floor. The then owner, Thomas Dight, is said to have returned home unexpectedly from London to find his mistress (not his wife, you'll notice) in bed with another man. In a psychotically jealous rage, he had the girl manacled and cut out her 'lying tongue'. Then he forced her to watch as he roasted her lover to death over a fire. After his rival's demise, Dight locked his unfortunate mistress in the room and left her to die of grief and starvation.

It is the girl's ghost who makes her presence known in the Old Mint House. Her apparition is described as 'a young woman in an old-fashioned close-fitting bodice with tight sleeves and a dress very full at the waist, with a small ruff around her neck'.

To close this chapter mention can be made of two more fortifications even older than the Roman walls at Pevensey. **Chanctonbury Ring** and **Cissbury Ring**, both on the South Downs Way in West Sussex, are Iron Age hill-forts that are thousands of years old. The 'rings' refer to the enclosing ramparts surrounding each hilltop monument. Once upon a time these defences would probably have been enhanced with wooden palisade walls and entrance towers but these are, of course, long gone.

A wide range of strange legends have built up around Chanctonbury Ring, with its distinctive stand of beech trees, planted in 1760. One old yarn is that the fort was constructed by the Devil and that he would offer supplicants a bowl of soup for their soul – not much of a bargain, in my opinion. In ages past, young married women would come to sleep on the hill believing that it would increase their fertility.

Another superstition is that if you run anti-clockwise (or 'widdershins') twelve times round the ramparts, the soul of a long-dead Druid will be conjured up. At night strange lights have been seen glowing in the centre of the hill-fort and also above it – Chanctonbury is something of a UFO hot-spot. Sudden unexpected feelings of panic have also been experienced by people walking through the Ring. Panic in lonely places was thought by the Greeks to indicate the presence of the hoofed god Pan (hence its name). Chanctonbury Ring certainly seems to be a place of ancient mystery, which might explain why the Romans built two temples within its ramparts after it was abandoned by the Britons.

The trig point on haunted Cissbury Ring. One of the ramparts on the haunted hill-fort can be seen curving round in the background.
Shutterstock/ Chester Tugwell

Cissbury Ring is another fascinating place. Encompassing an area of sixty acres, it is the second largest Iron Age hill-fort in England. It too has a connection with the Devil, for legend has it the hill was created by His Satanic Majesty as spoil while he was fiendishly digging a ditch which he hoped would let in the sea and drown Sussex. The sun rose before he could accomplish his wicked plan, however. Cissbury Ring is haunted by a highwayman who was hanged on its summit. His rather romantic wraith has been seen on moonlit nights, mounted on a splendid steed.

HOLY GHOSTS

There are a surprising number of haunted churches in East and West Sussex, as well as ecclesiastical ruins. One of these is St Peter's Church, Preston Village, in **Brighton** (near the very haunted Preston Manor). Women dressed in the fashions of the Middle Ages have been seen emerging from the south side of the church and then pottering through the graveyard. They vanish as they pass through a tombstone. A spectral horse canters round Brighton's St Nicholas's Church before galloping away. A horse's skeleton has been found buried deep in the churchyard and it is thought that its presence might be sacrificial. A ghostly nun is also said to wander near the church. All Saints, Patcham, is haunted by an unhappy looking woman who always appears to be shivering. Her identity is unknown.

The odd thing about the ghost of St Mary's, **Westham**, close to Pevensey Castle, is that it is so mundane. Described as wearing 'an ordinary grey suit', the figure appears to be of modern date. The ghost has been seen strolling along the path up to the church door. The figure looks so solid and ordinary that witnesses fail to suspect anything unusual about the man until he vanishes before their astonished eyes.

The church of St Thomas the Martyr at **Winchelsea** is especially picturesque because it was formerly the size of a small cathedral and the ruins of the larger building gather round what remains. The apparition of a black man in a red jacket haunts the churchyard. It's unknown who he is but it's possible that in life he was a footman at a nearby grand house. Caribbean slaves were fashionable in the 18th century.

An unknown black man haunts the churchyard at Winchelsea.
Shutterstock/ Lance Bellers

The ruin of a Franciscan monastery can also be found at Winchelsea. Two highwaymen formerly used the ruin as a base of operations and their ghosts are supposed to gallop round the district. Ghost-hunter Andrew Green reported hearing thundering hooves approaching him up the road to Rye near the monastery. Suddenly the hoofbeats stopped. The road remained empty and Green saw no horses to account for the sounds as he continued along it.

Switching to West Sussex now, and the church of St Andrew in **Steyning** is said to be haunted by Milian, a 13th-century parishioner who plagued the local clergy and continued to bother them after her death. Ghostly singing has been heard inside St Andrew's Church, **Didling**. A similar phenomenon, the chanting of long-dead monks, has been

If you see a strange white bird perched on the restored spire of Chichester Cathedral, don't tell the bishop. Shutterstock/ ian woolcock

heard at St Nicholas's Church, **Poling**, and at a nearby farm which used to be part of a priory. The spectral knight who marches with a regal air around Holy Trinity Church, **Bosham**, is thought by some to be the ghost of Harold Godwinson, the last Saxon king of England. When ancient human remains were discovered beneath the chancel in 1950, it was speculated that they might have belonged to King Harold, the theory being that after the fateful battle of 1066 his body was smuggled away and secretly buried here.

The Cathedral Church of **Chichester** was originally founded by the Normans in the 12th century after it was clear the old cathedral at Selsey was about to get washed into the sea. A series of fires, lightning strikes and problems with subsidence led to a number of later rebuilds, including the addition of a central spire despite these risks. In 1861 subsidence got the better of the cathedral again and the spire collapsed. This was slightly disconcerting, because an old saying had it that 'When Chichester steeple falls, there will be no King in England.' However, this was right in the middle of Queen Victoria's reign, making the omen somewhat redundant. The spire was replaced.

Another piece of folklore states that if a ghostly white bird (or more prosaically a heron) is seen to perch on Chichester Cathedral's spire, it is a warning of the imminent death of the current bishop. Two more traditional ghosts haunt the cathedral grounds. One is of an old man, the other of a monk. The latter is seen wandering about near the Minster House.

The grand Gothic Revival Cathedral Church of **Arundel** was built in 1873 with money donated by the 15th Duke of Norfolk. It was designed by the man who also designed that iconic mode of Victorian transport, the Hansom cab. Unfortunately, plans for a spire never materialised, but it is still an impressive structure. In 1899, the Bishop of Southwark, the Revd John Butt, retired and came to live in a room in Arundel Cathedral. The shade of Bishop Butt has been seen from time to time in the cathedral, sitting in a chair or on the stairs leading up to the room he once occupied.

Arundel's parish church is the 13th-century church of St Nicholas. Here the ghost of 'a white-haired woman in a long blue gown' has been seen – and possibly photographed – kneeling by the altar. The apparition may be linked to a statue of an Elizabethan woman in the church which researcher Arron Weedall states makes some people feel 'cold and uncomfortable'. Or the ghost may be that of a nun from a nearby convent. When a local solicitor photographed the interior of the church in the 1940s, one of the negatives later revealed the image of someone kneeling at the altar. There was certainly no one visible when he took the photo. The image is too blurry to determine whether the kneeling figure is that of a woman: it might just easily be that of a priest wearing a surplice. It's an intriguing mystery.

Michelham Priory, near Upper Dicker, was founded by the Augustinian order in 1229. After the Dissolution of the Monasteries, it was converted into a dwelling and remained a private home for centuries. It was restored in the 20th century and then presented to the Sussex Archaeological

Society, which still looks after it. Michelham Priory is in an excellent state of preservation and a fascinating glimpse not only into the life of a monastic order but also a Tudor country house. It is also a paranormally busy place.

The ghosts of Michelham Priory include a medieval canon who haunts the gatehouse, a riderless white horse which clatters through the gateway and a woman who walks a little dog on a lead through the grounds. There is the also the sad wraith of a woman whose child drowned in the moat and which has been seen sitting gazing hopelessly into the water. A double ghost was witnessed in the 1960s. A man in a cloak was seen to descend diagonally down from the ceiling in one of the downstairs rooms before gliding through a doorway. A woman in Tudor dress swiftly followed him. It would seem the ghostly couple had descended a staircase that had long since been taken out.

David Scanlan, author of *Paranormal Sussex*, has made a particular study of Michelham. A few years ago a live-in manager of the property explained to Mr Scanlan how his scepticism regarding the paranormal had been challenged by his own experience. Woken by the sound of something moving about one night, he got up to find that a great lump of furniture had shifted about the room, making a figure-of-eight pattern on the floor with one of its castors. On another occasion, he'd just locked up and was returning to the private accommodation when he passed a man on the stairs. A flight further up, it occurred to him that the visitor wouldn't be able to get out, so he hurried back down the stairs. The stairs and stairwell were empty. The visitor had somehow succeeded in vanishing through a locked and bolted door, for which only the manager had the key.

Mr Scanlan both saw and heard a rather shocking ghost at the Priory during an investigation by the Hampshire Ghost Club in 2004. In an article for *Paranormal Magazine*, he explained: 'Coming through the main entrance, I was confronted by the ghost of a brown-clad monk standing at the foot of staircase. The monk raised his right hand and pointed upstairs. He then shouted in a very loud voice, "He is a sick bastard!" before vanishing. Another member of the team entered seconds later but unfortunately didn't see or hear anything.'

Haunted Michelham Priory.
© Elaine Baker

The great abbey at **Battle** was founded by William the Conqueror in 1066 as a tribute to God for his victory over Harold I and also to show off. Supposedly, Battle Abbey was erected on the precise location where the Saxon and Norman armies met (hence its name), with the high altar set up on the place where King Harold fell. The Abbey Church is now in ruins and a fir tree marks the location of the altar. Hundreds of thousands of people visit the site of the Battle of Hastings every year but there have been challenges as to whether this is in fact the true location. The most recent came in 2013, when Channel 4's *Time Team* programme carried out a 'lidar' survey which revealed the original topography of the landscape and demonstrated that the only likely place for the showdown was a spot now occupied by a roundabout in Battle's town centre. Even English Heritage, who make a few bob out of visitors to the supposed battlefield, admitted they were impressed by the findings.

Nothing could shake your trust in the traditional site if you believed the local folklore, however. Legend has it that a fountain of blood spurted out of the ground where King Harold fell, testament to the quantity of Christian blood spilled here. A ghostly re-enactment of this gory miracle is said to still be seen from time to time. And that's not all. Sounds of fierce fighting and the apparition of running soldiers are also reported from the vicinity.

The ghost of Harold himself is also allegedly to be seen, struggling with an arrow in his eye. The arrow-in-eye hypothesis for the Saxon king's death comes from the Bayeux Tapestry but it is now thought that the picture of this unlucky soldier is not intended to represent Harold at all,

A phantom monk has been seen making its way towards the magnificent gatehouse of Battle Abbey.
Shutterstock/ Lance Bellers

and the idea that this is how he died has been largely discredited. The story that a ghostly man with an eye-patch can be seen staring out of a window in the abbey's gatehouse should not perhaps be taken seriously.

Slightly better attested are the accounts of a spectral knight glimpsed in the Common House. He has been seen by a number of visitors. On one occasion, a youngster who was with his parents on a guided tour suddenly called out: 'Who is that man with the long sword?' He seemed genuinely confused that neither his father, nor anyone else in the crowd, could see the armoured figure. The ghost of an old man in a leather jerkin and apron, who is thought to be a farrier, has been reported from the same part of the building.

A more commonly observed apparition is that of a monk. He has been seen near the abbey's Guest House and in the street making his way towards the gatehouse. Two further phantom monks, one in a black habit, the other in a cream-and-black habit, are known to potter together down a yew-lined walk beside the boundary wall.

The remaining ghosts of Battle Abbey are of women. This may seem surprising, in the context of a monastic house on or near an old battlefield, but it too suffered under the Dissolution of the Monasteries and became a private dwelling in the 16th century. Even to this day part of the abbey buildings is used as a school. The ghosts are distinguished by the colour of the dress they are seen wearing: one in grey, the other in red. The Grey Lady walks with a pronounced limp along a corridor connecting the Great Hall with the Abbot's House. The woman in red has been seen among the ruins and also on a staircase in the school. One witness who has seen her recognised her red gown as dating from the Elizabethan period. Sometimes the ghost is not seen but the swish of her silk dress is heard ascending the stairs.

In the 19th century, a Lady Webster stayed at Battle Abbey soon after she was married. She had retired for the night when suddenly her bed-curtains were pulled back and she found herself being glared at by 'an old woman of terrifying appearance'. Lady Webster lay speechless under the cold regard of the stranger. Then the hag turned away, dropping the curtain. Moments later, Lady Webster's husband strolled into the room. She asked him who on earth the old woman was. She'd assumed it was some aged servant. But her husband told her no one had left the room as he'd approached or entered and no one answering the woman's distinctive appearance was familiar to him at the abbey. This latter fact was confirmed by Lady Webster's own investigation the following morning and she came to the conclusion that her nocturnal visitor had been something unearthly.

GHOSTS OF COAST AND COUNTRY

Beachy Head, near Eastbourne, is one of the highest cliffs along the southern English coastline, a dramatic white chalk cliff standing 162 metres (530 feet) high. Beachy Head has an unenviable reputation of being a magnet for people wishing to end their lives. The number of suicides that have taken place here is said to be due to the cliff's great height and its accessibility from major towns, including London. But there has been speculation over a much stranger and more sinister reason for all these untimely deaths,

For decades there have been rumours of a malevolent spirit which lures, wills or pushes people over the cliff. The ghostly black monk glimpsed from time to time on Beachy Head is said to have been thrown to his death by officers of King Henry VIII during the Dissolution of the Monasteries. His spirit now seeks revenge. Andrew Green spoke to a police sergeant who confirmed that there is 'something really weird on the cliff top. It seems to make the most intrepid person liable to become dizzy or frightened.'

Paranormal researcher, the late T.C. Lethbridge, was convinced some places could be haunted by an invisible, malevolent presence that willed people to kill themselves. He called such entities 'ghouls' and believed his wife encountered one on a cliff top in Devon. He said she 'had the unpleasant experience of hearing, or appearing to hear, something saying: "Wouldn't you like to jump over?"' Perhaps a 'ghoul', be it the phantom monk or otherwise, is operating at Beachy Head.

Beachy Head has a notorious reputation for suicides and possibly the ghosts of suicides. Shutterstock/Andrei Nekrassov

It's possible that several of the other ghosts encountered on Beachy Head may be the ghosts of suicides themselves. A 'white, misty figure' has been seen drifting along the cliff's edge before suddenly disappearing, as if it had dropped over. Then there's the apparition of a woman who steps over the edge, taking with her a bundle thought to be a baby. A dog-walker along the top of the cliff one day met a woman whom he described as wearing an old-fashioned grey dress. He had no idea she was a ghost, but his corgi did – when the 'woman' bent down as if to stroke him, he ran away howling. The woman in grey then promptly vanished.

A particular eerie place is **Glydwish Wood** near Rudyard Kipling's old home, Bateman's (see 'The Grander Haunted Houses' chapter). Kipling described the wood as being 'full of a sense of ancient ferocity and evil'. He continued: 'I have sometimes … felt a secretive and menacing feeling all around me, holding me expectant and always on guard. Yes, and in this evil wood everything is evil.' Glydwish Wood is believed to be haunted by the angry ghost of David Leary, who was wrongfully hanged after the death of a neighbour in the wood. The author R. Thurston Hopkins recounted a horrifying encounter with Leary's ghost in his book *Adventures With Phantoms*. A witness told him Leary's raggedy form chased him through the trees, choking and moaning and plucking at his neck.

Nor is Glydwish the only stretch of woods in West Sussex with a sinister reputation. **Clapham Woods**, near Worthing, has been the focus of murder and mysterious disappearances for many years and abounds in rumours of black magic rituals carried out in dark groves even today. In

Ghosts and other strange phenomena have been reported from both Glydwish and Clapham Woods in West Sussex. Shutterstock/andreiuc88

their book *The Demonic Connection*, authors Toyne Newton, Charles Walker and Alan Brown highlighted a range of paranormal activity in Clapham Woods. Strange lights have been glimpsed among the trees and UFOs above them. One night a rambler on the vantage point of Highdown Hill saw a large glowing orange ball hover over the woods and then descend among the tree-tops.

'Misty grey shapes' have regularly been reported suddenly appearing in front of walkers in Clapham Woods, sometimes accompanied by a feeling of dread. One of these apparitions was so large it resembled a great, bulky bear. To cap off all these phenomena, ramblers through the woods have also reported being knocked over by invisible forces.

On the aforementioned **Highdown Hill** can be found the last resting place of a true English eccentric. A good number of years before his death in 1793, John Oliver built his own tomb on the side of the hill. Beside it he erected a summerhouse, where he would relax and enjoy the view of the surrounding countryside and this memento of his own mortality. He also had his coffin – a white one – made in advance – but kept it under his bed and used it to store bread and cheese. His eventual funeral was apparently a splendid one.

After Oliver's death, the tomb entered local ghost-lore. Generations of local children were told that if they ran around the tomb seven times, Oliver's ghost would leap out and chase them (although why anyone would want such an experience I can't imagine). The tradition was probably born out of the disapproval of countryfolk at Oliver choosing to be buried in ground that was not consecrated. They imagined, no doubt, that his spirit could not rest easy in such an unorthodox grave.

During his lifetime Oliver would certainly have known about a crime which took place at the West Sussex village of **Burpham**. In 1771 a villain called Jack Upperton, together with another man, set upon a post-boy in Blakehurst Lane just outside the village. The robbery failed and Upperton was apprehended. The other assailant escaped. Upperton was executed for the attempted robbery and his body was hung in chains where Burpham New Down meets Blakehurst Lane. A century after the gibbet was erected it had all but rotted away, along with Jack Upperton's remains. However, that did not stop the place from being avoided by the locals after dark. They were convinced the criminal's restless spirit still lingered there. Nan Tuck's Lane near **Buxted** in East Sussex is haunted by a woman who was pursued by an angry mob because they thought she was a witch. They chased her down the lane which now bears her name and here, sometime later, her body was found hanging from the stout branch of a tree. Some say Nan hanged herself to escape what she feared might be an even more violent fate. It seems more likely that she was lynched. Her ghost has been seen drifting along Nan Tuck's Lane, a dark grey shadow.

Finally, we move back to West Sussex and to the picturesque village of **Slindon**. Many of Slindon's charming brick-and-flint cottages are owned by the National Trust, and some of the surrounding countryside, too. A past tragedy has created the unusual haunting of Slindon. In the lanes and fields round about the village a riderless white horse has been seen and heard galloping furiously. One witness saw the horse galloping over fields beyond Mill Lane. She stopped to watch

The pretty countryside round Slindon is haunted by a galloping white horse.
Shutterstock/ Dave Porter

it and was astonished to see the animal disappear into thin air. Others have merely heard the phantom's thundering hooves. Riders have pulled in to let the other rider pass, only to realise that the lane is empty behind them.

The story told to account for the haunting is a sad one. A young stable lad took out a spirited white horse and set it recklessly galloping down the lanes. He failed to see a low branch and was killed. The frenzied animal charged about the countryside until it finally found its way back to its stable. Its empty saddle spoke volumes and the stable-hand's body was eventually located where it had fallen.